Doodle Stitching
THE MOTIF COLLECTION

Doodle Stitching

THE MOTIF COLLECTION

Aimee Ray

400+ easy embroidery designs

LARK CRAFTS
A Division of Sterling Publishing Co., Inc.
New York / London

Senior Editor: Nicole McConville

Editorial Assistant: Beth Sweet

Art Director: Kathleen Holmes

Junior Designer: Carol Morse

Illustrator: Aimee Ray

Photography Director: Dana Irwin

Photographer: Lynne Harty

Cover Designer: Celia Naranjo

Library of Congress Cataloging-in-Publication Data

Ray, Aimee, 1976-
Doodle stitching : the motif collection : 400+ easy embroidery designs / Aimee Ray. -- 1st ed.
    p. cm.
  Includes index.
  ISBN 978-1-60059-581-3 (pb with cd : alk. paper)
  1. Embroidery--Patterns. 2. Stitches (Sewing) I. Title.
  TT771.R374 2010
  746.44--dc22

                          2010008607

10 9 8 7 6 5 4 3 2 1

First Edition

Published by Lark Crafts, A Division of Sterling Publishing Co., Inc.
387 Park Avenue South, New York, NY 10016

Text © 2010, Aimee Ray

Photography © 2010, Lark Crafts, A Division of Sterling Publishing Co., Inc.

Illustrations © 2010, Aimee Ray

Distributed in Canada by Sterling Publishing, c/o Canadian Manda Group, 165 Dufferin Street
Toronto, Ontario, Canada M6K 3H6

Distributed in the United Kingdom by GMC Distribution Services,
Castle Place, 166 High Street, Lewes, East Sussex, England BN7 1XU

Distributed in Australia by Capricorn Link (Australia) Pty Ltd.,
P.O. Box 704, Windsor, NSW 2756 Australia

If you have questions or comments about this book, please contact:
Lark Books
67 Broadway
Asheville, NC 28801
828-253-0467

Manufactured in China

ISBN 13: 978-1-60059-581-3

For information about custom editions, special sales, and premium and
corporate purchases, please contact Sterling Special Sales Department at
800-805-5489 or specialsales@sterlingpub.com.

For information about desk and examination copies available to college and
university professors, requests must be submitted to academic@larkbooks.com.
Our complete policy can be found at www.larkbooks.com.

Contents

Introduction

Find the stitch guide to this doodle stitch on www.larkbooks.com/bonus

Doodle stitching is just as playful and easy and enchanting as it sounds. It's my no-pressure approach to embroidery, infusing centuries-old embroidery techniques with a fresh spirit of experimentation and designs you can mix and match. My first book, *Doodle Stitching*, introduced the concept, and the response was huge. I took that as a sign that embroidery, especially when it incorporates an imaginative style, is here to stay. Crafters of all skill levels see it as one of the easiest—and most addictive—ways to transform ordinary objects into personalized pieces graced with handmade charm and creativity.

The most resounding response I received from the first book was that readers wanted more, more, more. And here it is! You'll find an expanded and updated version of all the embroidery basics of the first book, plus a collection of more than 400 embroidery motifs organized into more than a dozen categories I thought would meet your stitching needs and spark your imagination. Looking for something for a baby shower or birthday celebration? Check. What about designs to celebrate your passion for flowers or irresistibly cute critters? Got it. Or maybe an alphabet to craft monograms or a variety of embellishments to freshen up last season's frock? That's here, too.

Kick your doodling up to the next level using the enclosed CD to enlarge, edit, or combine motifs to your heart's content. And whether you do that or use motifs straight from the pages of the book, I'll walk you step-by-step through four easy options of transferring motifs to any sort of surface.

Still want more? You'll find 17 brand new projects that showcase some of the motifs in the collection. You can follow them stitch-by-stitch, or, better yet, use them as a creative springboard for your own doodle stitch creations.

So grab your needle and some floss, and let's get started!

Embroidery Essentials

Embroidery requires only a few basic, inexpensive tools and materials that you can find at any craft store or even in your own stash of craft supplies. All you really need to get started is a needle, floss, hoop, and some fabric, but there are a few other items that will come in handy as well. Read through this section before you get started, and become familiar with the tools of the trade and how to use them.

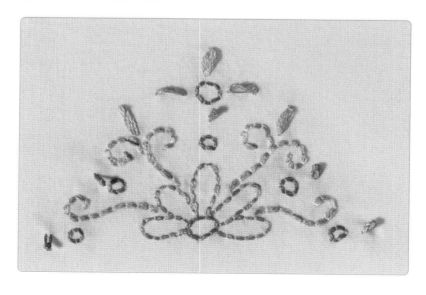

Materials & Tools

Floss

You can embroider with just about any thread or string, but what is most commonly used is embroidery floss. It comes in any color you want (and many more) in small bundles, or skeins. A strand of floss is made up of six threads, or plies, twisted together. For a thick embroidered line, you can use all six. For smaller, more delicate work, you can separate the threads and use less. I use either six or three threads for most embroidery projects, and often one thread for hand-sewing fabrics together.

Standard cotton floss is most common, but there are also many specialty flosses available, such as metallic, linen, silk, and gradient colors, which are fun to play with.

I'm not a neat freak by any means, but I do love to organize. When my creative space and supplies are arranged to where I can easily see and find everything, I feel much more inspired to make things and use all the crafty stuff I've collected. There are lots of ways to organize your floss and lots of products on the market to help you. Personally, I use a clear plastic fishing tackle box, and homemade cardboard bobbins. Here's what my storage box looks like.

Each skein of embroidery floss comes wrapped in paper with a different number for each color. When you unwrap a new skein of floss,

Embroidery Toolbox

Embroidery hoop
(a 6-inch [15.2 cm] circle is a good one to start with)

Embroidery and sewing needles

Embroidery floss

Fabric stabilizer

Iron

Nonpermanent fabric pen

Sewing scissors

Straight pins

Thimble

Transfer or tracing tools

Tweezers

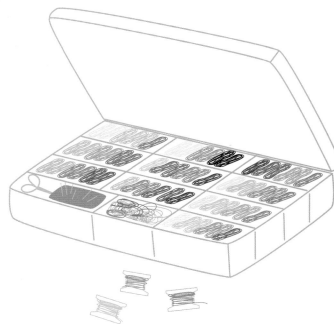

it's a good idea to keep track of the number on the package. There are hundreds of different floss colors, and you may think you'll remember that specific shade of green you ran out of when you get to the store, only to come home and realize you were way off. (I've done this.) So, make it easy by winding floss onto a cardboard bobbin and writing the number on it. Here is the template I use to make mine.

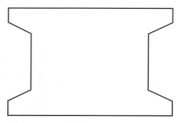

I keep all my floss bobbins in a 9 x 14-inch (22.9 x 35.6 cm) clear plastic tackle box, arranged by color. I have one extra slot in the box for leftover floss pieces that are too long to throw away, and another for my scissors and a small pincushion with pins and needles. I can easily close the box up and put it away when I'm not using it (though usually it sits open on the couch in the living room, along with my current project) or even take it with me to use on the road.

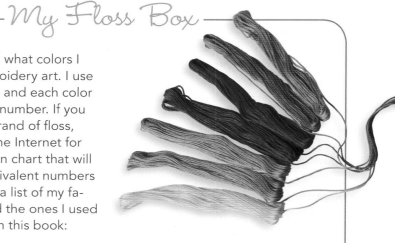

My Floss Box

Color Palette

I often get asked what colors I used in my embroidery art. I use DMC brand floss and each color is labeled with a number. If you use a different brand of floss, you can search the Internet for a color conversion chart that will give you the equivalent numbers to these. Here is a list of my favorite colors, and the ones I used for the projects in this book:

Pink: dark 760, medium 761, light 3713

Cherry Red: 321/304

Coral: dark 350 through light 353

Coral Red: 349

Orange: dark 720, medium 721, light 722

Yellow orange: 3854

Yellow: 727

Pale Green: dark 3346 through light 3348

Bright Green: dark 905, medium 906, light 907

Aqua: medium 3811, light 747

Turquoise: dark 3810, medium 597, light 598

Blue: dark 340, medium 341/157, light 3747

Plum: dark 3834, medium 3835, light 3836

Brown: dark 433 through light 437

Yellow brown: medium 676, light 422,

Ecru

Black: 310

White: Blanc

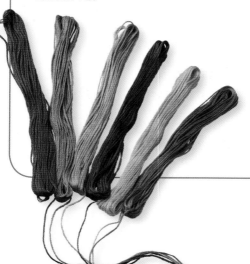

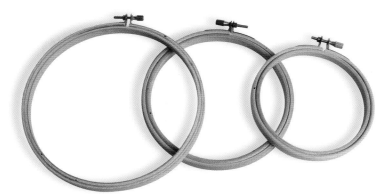

Needles

There is really no special size or type of needle you have to use for embroidering. All you really need is one with a sharp point and a hole, or eye, large enough for you to thread easily. You will probably want a needle with a larger eye if you're using all six threads of floss, and one with a small eye if you're using three or less, or hand-sewing with thread. I like to buy packs of several different sizes of needles so I have a variety to choose from. Keep a small pincushion close by so your needles won't get lost. You can easily make one of any shape or size by hand-sewing two pieces of felt together with a little stuffing inside. Don't forget to decorate it with embroidery!

Embroidery Hoops

Although you can embroider some heavy, thick fabrics without a hoop, most fabrics will require one. Hooping your fabric will give you a tight, smooth surface to stitch on, and it will prevent puckering. Embroidery hoops have two round frames that fit together and tighten with a screw. The frames hold your fabric tightly between them as you stitch. They come in plastic or wood and many different sizes. Plastic hoops are a good investment; they are sturdier than wood and will last a long time. You can use different sized hoops for different sized projects, but I've found a 6-inch (15.2 cm) one works well for almost anything.

Fabric and More

You can embroider on any fabric or material you can stick a needle through. The most common, and the fabric used for many of the projects in this book, is quilter's cotton. Felt, canvas, denim, and satin are also great fabrics to embroider on. Try embroidering your clothes, dish towels, pillowcases, or any other fabric you find needing a little added interest.

You may not have thought about embroidering other surfaces besides fabric, but heavy paper, vinyl, thin plastics, and even balsa wood can also be embroidered. To stitch on balsa wood, first apply a layer of glue and a thin

Thimble

A thimble is nice to have when stitching heavy fabrics like canvas or denim. A leather or rubber one will make gripping and pushing the needle through the fabric much easier on your fingers.

Scissors

Any pair of scissors will do, but it's nice to have a small pair of sharp sewing scissors that you can keep with your embroidery floss and supplies.

Transferring Patterns

cotton fabric to the back to prevent cracking. When stitching on wood or paper, you'll want to poke holes from the front first to come through from the back. It's best to stick with simpler stitches, and to not pull through so tightly that the paper rips or balsa wood cracks. With a little extra care, you can make lots of unique projects with embroidery on these surfaces.

Stabilizer

When embroidering on stretchy or delicate fabrics such as T-shirt cotton or silk, you will want to use a fabric stabilizer. Stabilizer comes in many varieties: The type I use most is the tear-away paper kind with an adhesive back. You can easily cut it to whatever size or shape you need, stick it onto the back of your fabric, and remove and re-position it if necessary. You will then stitch through the paper and fabric together. After you're done, just tear away the excess. Use tweezers to remove any bits of paper caught under the stitches. For delicate fabrics, choose a water-soluble stabilizer that will simply dissolve in water when you're done embroidering.

There are several methods for transferring embroidery designs and patterns to fabric. Different ways work better for different types of fabric. It's a good idea to test any fabric pens or iron-on prints on a piece of scrap fabric to be sure they will work for you.

Light Method

The method I use most is tracing patterns using a light table or a sunny window. Tape your pattern to a table or window and secure the fabric over it so you can see the pattern lines through the fabric. My favorite tools for tracing pattern lines onto fabric are water-soluble fabric markers. Fabric marker lines are easy to remove with water when you're done embroidering. An ordinary pencil will work too, although it is more difficult to remove. Just be sure you cover lead pencil lines completely with your embroidery. This method works best for lightweight, light-colored fabrics.

Carbon Paper Method

Another way to transfer patterns to fabric is by using fabric carbon paper. It comes in a variety of colors to contrast the color of fabric you're using. Place your fabric on a hard surface, set a piece of carbon paper face down on top of it, and your pattern on top of that. Trace the pattern lines with a pencil or other blunt object, such as a knitting needle. I use this method mostly for darker colored fabrics that marker lines don't show up on.

Iron-On Transfers

A third method is to make an iron-on transfer. You can do this by making a black and white laser print or photocopy of any design. Remember, especially if your pattern includes text, that you'll need to reverse the image before printing it because it will be backwards when you apply it to your fabric. Simply place the print on top of your fabric face down and iron it on. The lines will be permanent, though they may fade with washing or over time, so you'll want to cover them completely with your embroidery. You can reuse your iron-on print several times.

Tissue Paper Method

One more transferring technique is to trace your pattern onto thin paperlike tissue or tracing paper, pin the paper to your fabric, and stitch right through the paper and the fabric together. When you're done, just tear away the paper. Use tweezers or the tip of your needle to remove any bits of paper caught under the stitches. This method works well for thick fabrics like felt, which can be tricky to transfer onto any other way.

The CD included with this book conveniently gives you all the motifs in digital form as black and white TIFF files, so you can use them however you like. Just pop it in your computer, read the helpful User Guide, and you'll quickly be on your way. You can resize them in any image editing program, print them out, and transfer them to your fabric using one of the methods described. Remember, if you're using the laser print/photocopy iron-on method, you'll need to reverse your images first so they don't come

out backwards. You will most often want to use black line art for easy transferring.

Take advantage of having all the motifs in digital form by combining them into your own unique patterns and designs! Resize, overlap, change colors, omit image elements, or draw in your own additions to make a pattern distinctly yours. If you are proficient with your image program, you can design your own projects digitally before printing them, trying out lots of different colors

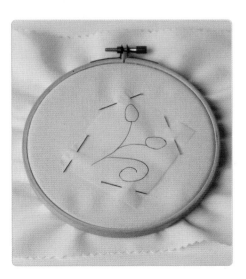

This design contains motifs 166, 431, 434.

Stitch Away

and layout options. If you're better with paper and scissors, print and cut out your favorite motifs and arrange them by hand, collage style. Remember, there are many stitch options using even one motif; you can use a variety of stitches in different ways. See the embroidered matryoshka dolls below. By combining several motifs from different

sections with your favorite stitches, colors, and your own imagination, you will discover endless possibilities. It's up to you to pick out what stitches you want to try, or to add extra details or textures that may not be included in the pattern. You can even leave things out if you want. That's why I like to use removable fabric markers, so I'm free to change my mind as I work and remove all the pattern lines when I'm finished. Feel free to experiment and add your own flair, and above all, just have fun.

After you've chosen your motifs, transferred your pattern to fabric, and applied stabilizer (if needed), you will stretch the fabric onto a hoop. Place the fabric over the inside frame and the outer frame on top of that, fitting them together. Tighten the screw and gently pull the edges of the fabric so it's tight.

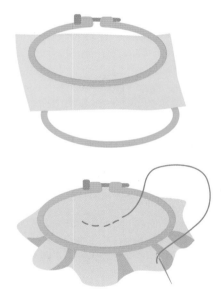

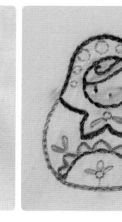

Next, choose a color of floss, cut a length about 12 inches (30.5 cm) long, and thread your needle. If you have trouble, try dampening one end of the floss and twisting it to a point. Tie a knot in the other end of the floss. One way to tie a knot is to wrap it around your finger, roll it off and pull downward to tighten it.

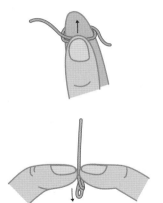

Now, the fun part: Start embroidering! Pull the needle and floss through from the back of your fabric until the knot catches. Now choose a stitch and follow the pattern's lines. When you finish a line or color section of embroidery stitches, or

you get down to about 2 inches (5.1 cm) of floss, you'll want to tie a small knot on the back by slipping your needle under a stitch, looping it and pulling it tight. Snip off the extra floss and start again.

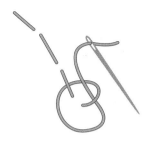

You can work on your embroidery section by section, completing each area before moving on to the next one, or, stitch a single color throughout the design before moving on to the next color.

Finishing Up

When you've finished your embroidery, remove the fabric from the hoop and erase any transfer lines by rinsing it with water or hand-washing it with a gentle detergent. Press the water out by spreading the fabric flat or rolling it between two towels. When it's almost dry, iron it face down on a towel. This will remove any wrinkles but prevent crushing your stitches.

The Back

Most of the time, I'm not too concerned with what the back of my embroideries look like, though they can turn out to be quite interesting and abstract! You may want to take extra care to keep your backs looking neat, if they will be visible, such as on a dish towel, or on very thin, light-colored fabrics where messy knots or tails of floss can show through the fabric. To keep the backs of your embroidery looking neat, tie your knots tightly and close to the fabric and snip off any extra floss right above the knot. Also, limit the distance you stretch your floss across the back from stitch to stitch. Tie off your floss with each section of the design and start with a new knot at the next point, rather than stretching your floss from point to point. I usually don't stretch my floss longer than ½ inch (3.8 cm); this reduces the "spider web" effect on the back.

Now that you've learned all about the tools and techniques used in embroidery, it's time to start stitching! Here are some basic embroidery stitches to get you started.

Straight Stitch

The Straight Stitch is the most basic embroidery stitch. Just pull your needle through from the back at A and push it back down at B. Straight Stitches can be any length, from a tiny dot to a line about ¼ inch (.6 cm) long. Make several Straight Stitches in a line to form the Running Stitch or in a circle pointing out from the center to make a flower shape. You can also stitch them individually or in groupings for small details like eyes or fur.

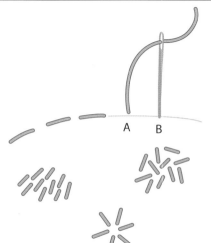

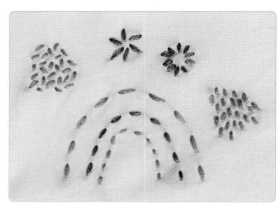

Cross Stitch

Start with a small diagonal Straight Stitch, from A to B. Make a second stitch over it from C to D. Rows of Cross Stitches look neater when the lines for each cross overlap in the same direction. If you're making a row, you can start by making a line of identical diagonal stitches, then going back and crossing them over the other direction.

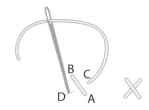

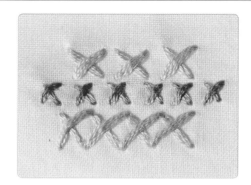

Star Stitch

Stars can be made in the same way as Cross Stitches. Start by making a Cross Stitch, and then add an additional Straight Stitch on top of it, from A to B.

Another way to make a Star is by making several Straight Stitches in a circle, ending at the same center point. Make your first stitch from A to B, your second stitch from C to B, and so on. Continue around the center adding as many stitches as you like until you reach the first stitch.

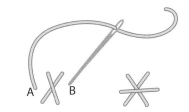

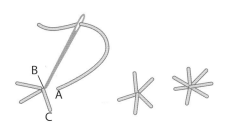

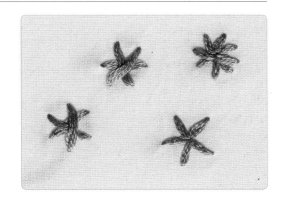

Split Stitch

Split Stitched lines are quick and easy to make, and make great outlines.

Make a small Straight Stitch from A to B. Bring the needle back up at C, splitting the first stitch in half. Continue making stitches and splitting them, to form a line.

Stem Stitch

The Stem Stitch is perfect for stitching curved lines or flower stems, which is how it got its name. Make a stitch from A to B, leaving the floss a little loose. Pull the needle to the front again at C, between A and B and just to one side. Pull the floss tight and continue to form a line of stitches.

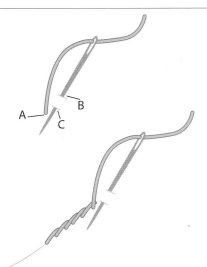

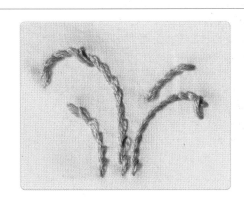

Back Stitch

The Back Stitch is a nice, clean outlining stitch. Start with a small stitch in the opposite direction, from A to B. Bring your needle back through the fabric at C, ahead of the first stitch and ending at A. Repeat to make each new Back Stitch, working backward on the surface and inserting the needle at the end of the previous stitch.

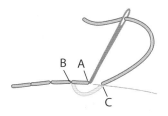

Chain Stitch

The Chain Stitch is great for a thick outline, but also works nicely as a decorative border. Pull the needle and floss through the fabric at A (figure 1). Insert the needle back in at A, pulling the floss through to the back until you have a small loop on the front. Bring the needle back up through the fabric inside of the loop at B (figure 2). Reinsert the needle at B, pulling the floss through to form a second small loop. Continue stitching loops to make a Chain (figure 3). When you finish a row, make a tiny stitch over the end of the last loop to hold it in place.

To end a Chain Stitch circle, stop one stitch short of the first stitch, and slide your needle and floss underneath it at C (figure 4). Then finish the last stitch, completing the circle.

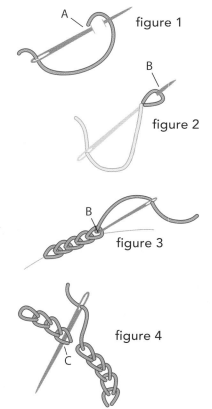

figure 1

figure 2

figure 3

figure 4

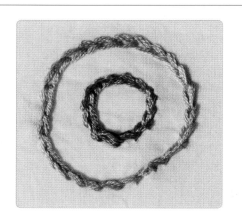

Blanket Stitch

The Blanket Stitch makes a great decorative border or edging. Make a loose, diagonal stitch from A to B. Bring the needle up again at C, catching the floss under the needle and pulling it tight to the fabric.

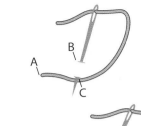

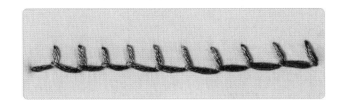

Herringbone Stitch

Herringbone Stitches are a variation on the Cross Stitch and make a unique looking decorative row. Start by making a diagonal stitch from A to B. Bring the needle back up at C, just to the left of the end of the first stitch. Reinsert the needle at D, and continue your Herringbone row.

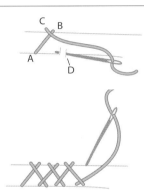

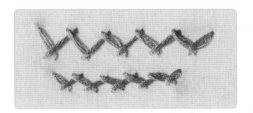

Threaded Running Stitch

Make a line of small, close Running Stitches and tie off the floss. Start a second floss strand, in another color, at the same spot as the first line of stitches, at A. Working only on the front of the fabric, slide the needle back and forth under each Running Stitch and then tie off this color at the end of the line. You can make a variety of pretty Threaded Running Stitches by weaving more than one color in different directions through the original Running Stitch.

Color 2

Color 1

French Knot

French Knots can be tricky at first, but they are well worth taking the time to learn. Individually, they make great dot accents, or fill an area solidly with French Knots for an interesting texture. Bring the needle through the fabric at A. Wrap the floss around the tip of the needle in the direction shown, and reinsert the needle at B, right next to A. Pull the floss tight and close to the fabric as you pull the needle back through. You can make larger French Knots by wrapping the floss around the needle multiple times.

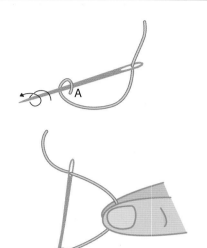

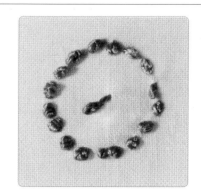

Lazy Daisy

The Lazy Daisy Stitch is the perfect way to make flower petals and leaves. You can use Satin Stitches or French Knots to make the flower centers. Bring your needle through the fabric at A and put it back down in the same spot, but don't pull the floss all the way through; leave a small loop. Now bring your needle back through the fabric inside the loop at B and back down at C, catching the loop at the top and securing it to the fabric. Repeat this stitch in a circle to make a daisy.

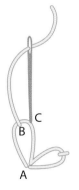

Feather Stitch

The Feather Stitch makes a unique border or decorative foliage. Make a loose diagonal stitch from A to B. Bring the needle back through the fabric next to B, at C, catching the previous stitch. Make another diagonal stitch in the other direction, at D Make your stitches back and forth to form a line.

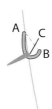

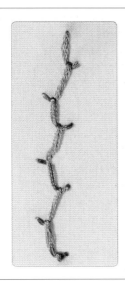

Fly Stitch

The Fly Stitch is an interesting decorative accent stitch and also makes cute flowers. Pair it with a Satin Stitch circle or French Knots to form the buds. Make a loose horizontal stitch from A to B. Press the loop flat to one side with your finger. Bring the needle back up at C, in the center of the first stitch. Return the needle at D, securing the first stitch to the fabric.

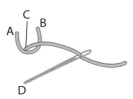

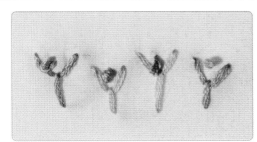

Scallop Stitch

The Scallop Stitch is a cousin to the Fly Stitch and Lazy Daisy and is made with the same basic technique. Scallop Stitches are also great for making flowers or leaves, or stitch several in a row to make a pretty border. Make a loose stitch from A to B and press it flat to one side with your finger. Bring the needle to the front of the fabric at C, inside the loop. Insert the needle at the outside of the stitch, at D, to hold it in place.

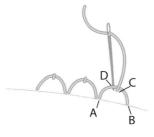

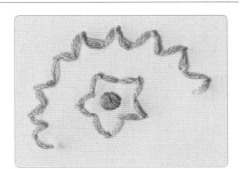

Satin Stitch

Satin Stitches are a lovely way to fill in small areas with smooth, solid color. Make a Straight Stitch from A to B. Make a second stitch right next to the first one from C to D. Always bring your needle up on one side and down on the other for best results. If you have trouble keeping the edges of your area even, first outline the shape with a tight Back Stitch or Split Stitch, and make your Satin Stitches over the top. For an extra smooth area of Satin Stitches, untwist and separate the threads of floss first.

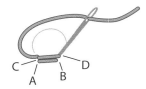

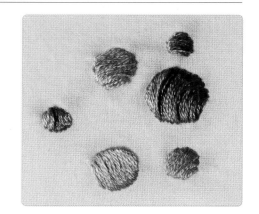

Long and Short Stitch

The Long and Short Stitch is used to cover large areas with solid or blended color. Start the first row by making a stitch from A to B. Next, make another stitch right next to it from C to D, only half as long. Repeat making a long stitch, then a short one to form the first row. Only the first row has both long and short stitches, the rest of the stitches will all be the same length. For the second row, make stitches just below your first row of stitches, filling in the spaces. Unless you're stitching a perfect square of Long and Short Stitches, they probably won't all be perfectly uniform, and that is just fine. Add a stitch here and there to fill in any gaps as you go along. Just keep your stitches all going in the same direction and you'll have an evenly filled area when you're finished.

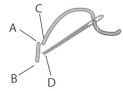

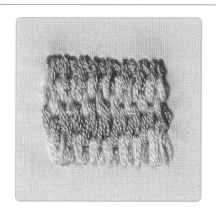

Sewing Essentials

Mastering a few easy sewing techniques can open you up to a world of simple sewing projects. Here are a few techniques used in the book's projects. They can easily be done by hand if you don't have a sewing machine.

Appliqué

Stitching a piece of contrasting colored or patterned fabric onto your embroidery fabric surface adds color and interest to your work.

Felt is a great fabric to use for appliqués. It is thick and easy to cut, and the edges don't fray. For a felt appliqué, just cut out the finished shape and stitch it onto the background fabric.

When using cotton or other fabric for appliqués, you can either use pinking shears for a decorative edge, or you can fold the edges under. Felt shapes or other fabric shapes cut with pinking shears can be added using any embroidery stitch or the Appliqué Stitch.

To hide fraying fabric edges, draw your shape onto the fabric, and cut it out, but leave ¼-inch (.6 cm) extra space beyond the lines. Press the ¼-inch (.6 cm) seam to the back of the appliqué shape and stitch it on with the Appliqué Stitch. Another technique especially good for shapes with curved edges is to cut a second

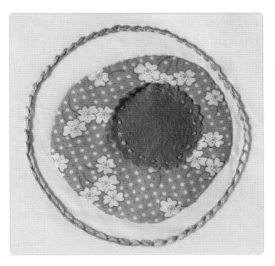

piece of fabric the same shape as your appliqué piece. Sew them together with right sides facing, leaving a 1-inch (2.5 cm) opening. Notch the edges, turn the piece right side out, and press it flat. Now the edges are neatly hidden and you can stitch the appliqué onto your fabric. You can even stuff the piece for a three-dimensional effect, or cut away the hidden fabric behind the appliqué if you want it flatter.

Appliqué Stitch

Pin the appliqué shape in place on the fabric background. Pull a knotted length of thread from the back of the background fabric to the front at A, very near the edge, and through the appliqué. Insert the needle back through the background fabric at B and bring the tip of the needle up again at C. Pull the thread tightly through, securing the fabrics together. Continue making even, equally spaced stitches around the perimeter of the appliqué.

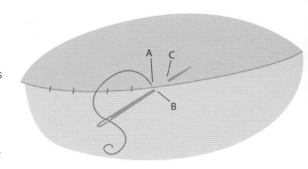

Embroidering with Beads

Beads add fun, sparkly accents to your embroidery. It's easy to stitch them on individually or in rows. Depending on the size of the beads you're using, you may be able to use a sewing needle, or you may need to purchase some extra thin beading needles, which will fit through the holes of even the tiniest beads. Use thread or one of the six threads of embroidery floss in a color matching your bead. Sew beads on one at a time using a small Straight Stitch, or three to four small beads at a time using the Back Stitch.

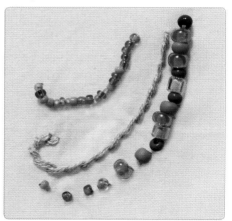

Double Hem

Your projects will look neat and professional with this hem. Just fold the edge of the fabric under twice and stitch it in place. To make a ½-inch (1.3 cm) double hem, fold the cut, or raw, fabric edge ½ inch (1.3 cm) to the underside and press. Now fold the edge under ½ inch (1.3 cm) again and sew along the top through all the layers of fabric.

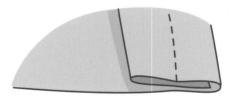

Hidden Stitch

This is a nearly invisible stitch used to close holes in pillows or toys after they're stuffed. Fold the excess fabric in along each side of the opening and pin the hole closed. Thread a needle with thread matching the color of the fabric and knot it at one end. Bring the needle and thread through the fabric from the back at A and back down directly across the opening at B. Slide the needle along the inside of the fold and pull it back out at C, trapping the stitch inside. Reinsert the needle across from C at D, pulling the thread tightly. Continue stitching along the opening, closing up the seam. When you get to the end, make a tiny knot buried in the seam.

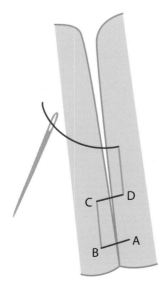

Topstitch

Topstitching is done by hand or machine after the fabric pieces are sewn together and the project is turned right side out. Just sew a line of small Straight Stitches close together through both layers of fabric. Topstitching is usually done close to and parallel with an edge.

Whip Stitch

Whip Stitches are a great way to add a decorative touch while joining pieces of fabric together along matched edges. You can also use it to hem the raw edge of a piece of fabric, or alone as a decorative stitch. Use matching thread to hide your stitches, or embroidery floss in a contrasting color to show them off.

Starting at the back, or between two pieces of fabric, bring your needle and floss through at A. Bring the needle over the edge of the fabric and reinsert it from the back at B.

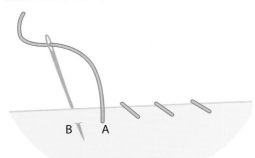

Notching Edges

When making projects such as pillows or stuffed toys, you will sew two pieces of fabric together with the right sides facing. Before you turn the fabric pieces right side out again, you will want to first "notch" the fabric around the seam so that the edges of your finished project look neat and smooth. For curved edges, cut small, triangular pieces out of the fabric, cutting right up to, but not through your stitched seam (figure 1). Make notches ½ to 1 inch (1.3 to 2.5 cm) apart. The tighter the curve, the more notches should be cut. Cut corners off straight across as shown (figure 2).

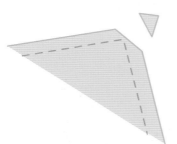

figure 1

figure 2

Projects

Sweet Baby Bodysuits

How can a baby be any cuter? Dressed up in an adorable embroidered outfit!

WHAT YOU NEED

Set of 3 white cotton baby bodysuits

Fabric stabilizer

Embroidery floss, 1 skein each of yellow, dark pink, medium pink, light turquoise, dark turquoise, light aqua, orange, and brown*

Motifs: 083, 092, 093

The author used DMC embroidery floss colors 727, 760, 761, 598, 747, 3810, 742, and 433.

STITCHES

French Knot

Lazy Daisy

Long Stitch

Short Stitch

Split Stitch

INSTRUCTIONS

1. Size the rattle and bottle motifs to 1½ inches (3.8 cm) tall and the duck to 1½ inches (3.8 cm) wide. Transfer one to the front of each bodysuit.

2. Cut a piece of stabilizer big enough to cover each design and apply it to the back of the fabric. My favorite stabilizer to use on cotton T-shirt fabric is a tear-away, sticky back type.

3. Hoop the fabric and stitch away! Begin by outlining each motif with the Split Stitch, then fill in each color section with the Long and Short Stitch. You might find it easiest to add details like the duck's eye and wing after you've filled in his body.

4. When you're done stitching, remove the excess stabilizer from the back. Now that cute baby can step out in style!

VARIATION

Many other motifs would work well here, from the peas in a pod and pumpkin on page 101 to any of the woodland animals on page 121.

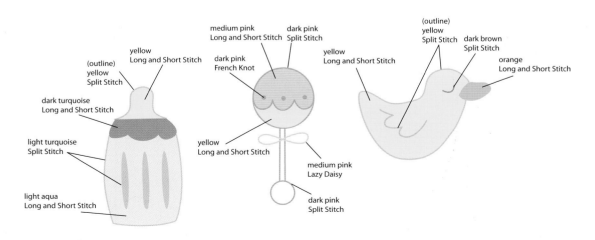

(outline)
yellow
Split Stitch

yellow
Long and Short Stitch

dark turquoise
Long and Short Stitch

light turquoise
Split Stitch

light aqua
Long and Short Stitch

medium pink
Long and Short Stitch

dark pink
Split Stitch

dark pink
French Knot

yellow
Long and Short Stitch

medium pink
Lazy Daisy

dark pink
Split Stitch

(outline)
yellow
Split Stitch

dark brown
Split Stitch

yellow
Long and Short Stitch

orange
Long and Short Stitch

Kitchen Coasters

Enjoy a little embroidery every morning with your coffee or tea.

WHAT YOU NEED

Cream cotton fabric, 3 circles, each 4 inches (10.2 cm)

Embroidery floss, 1 skein each of light turquoise, medium brown, dark brown, and medium yellow brown*

3 round, clear acrylic coasters that hold photos or embroidery, each 3 inches (7.6 cm)

Motifs: 246, 247, 321

The author used DMC embroidery floss colors 598, 435, 433, and 676.

STITCHES

French Knot

Lazy Daisy

Scallop Stitch

Stem Stitch

Straight Stitch

INSTRUCTIONS

1. Size the tea and coffee motifs to 2 inches (5.1 cm) wide or tall.

2. Use the coaster insert as a template to measure and mark three 3-inch (7.6 cm) circles on a piece of fabric, leaving at least ½ inch (1.3 cm) around the edges. Transfer an embroidery design to the center of each one and embroider them according to the pattern.

3. Cut out each circle leaving ½ inch (1.3 cm) of extra fabric around the edge. Follow the instructions on the package for inserting your embroidery into the coasters. You will wrap the fabric over the insert, secure it to the back, and fit it into the coaster.

VARIATION

Kick it up a notch using the beer stein, wine bottle and glass, or one of the cocktails on pages 99 and 100.

Tip

There are a variety of acrylic items available that will hold embroidery, such as key chains, magnets, frames, and mugs. It's easy to spread a little embroidery throughout your world!

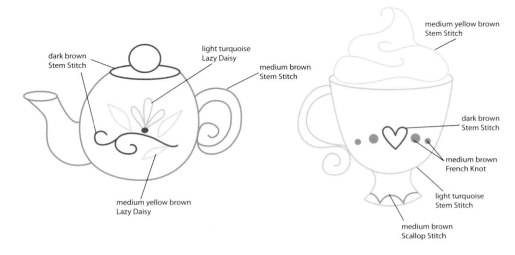

dark brown Stem Stitch

light turquoise Lazy Daisy

medium brown Stem Stitch

medium yellow brown Lazy Daisy

medium yellow brown Stem Stitch

dark brown Stem Stitch

medium brown French Knot

light turquoise Stem Stitch

medium brown Scallop Stitch

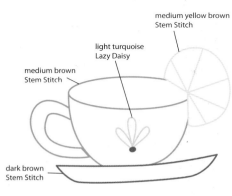

medium yellow brown Stem Stitch

light turquoise Lazy Daisy

medium brown Stem Stitch

dark brown Stem Stitch

Curtain Ties

Add a splash of decorative flair with these easy-to-sew curtain ties.

WHAT YOU NEED

Template (page 128)

Any fabric, 2 pieces for each tie, each 26 x 5 inches (66 x 12.7 cm)

Embroidery floss, 1 skein each of medium bright green and light bright green*

A variety of beads in coordinating colors

Motif: 171

The author used DMC embroidery floss colors 906 and 907.

STITCHES

Back Stitch

Chain Stitch

Satin Stitch

INSTRUCTIONS

1. Transfer the template to one half of one strip of fabric, flip it around and transfer it to the other end so that they match up in the middle.

2. Transfer the design to the fabric and embroider. Sew on the beads as shown.

3. Pin the two strips of fabric together with right sides facing and sew along the template line, leaving a 2-inch (5.1 cm) space open at the end. Turn it right side out, press, and stitch up the opening.

4. Gently tie or knot the tie around your curtain and pull it back with a nail or hook in the wall.

VARIATION

Any of the long, thin embellishments on pages 88-91 would work well here.

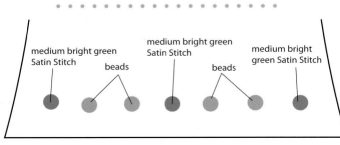

medium bright green Satin Stitch

beads

medium bright green Satin Stitch

beads

medium bright green Satin Stitch

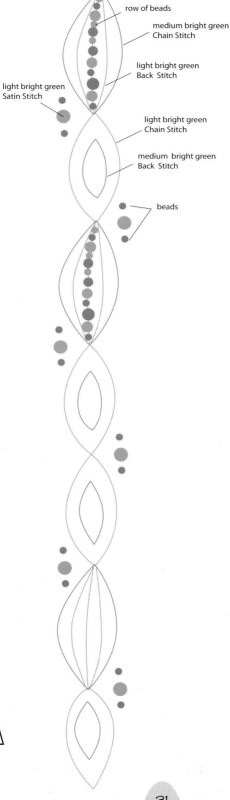

row of beads

medium bright green Chain Stitch

light bright green Back Stitch

light bright green Satin Stitch

light bright green Chain Stitch

medium bright green Back Stitch

beads

All-Weather Draft Dodger

Keep out the cold and save on energy bills with this cute and functional pillow.

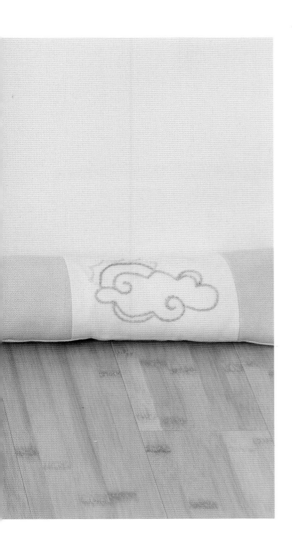

WHAT YOU NEED

Heavy white fabric (cotton or twill):

1 piece, 4 ½ x 36 inches (11.4 x 91.4 cm)

4 pieces, each 4 ½ x 6 inches (11.4 x 15.2 cm)

Heavy aqua fabric:

3 pieces, each 4½ x 4½ inches (11.4 x 11.4 cm)

2 pieces, each 4 ½ x 3½ inches (11.4 x 8.9 cm)

Embroidery floss, 1 skein each of medium blue, medium aqua, medium turquoise, light pale green, medium pink, yellow orange, and yellow*

Plastic beanbag pellets, dry rice, or beans

Polyester fiberfill stuffing

Motifs: 390, 392, 393, 398, 399

The author used DMC embroidery floss colors 341, 3811, 597, 3348, 761, 3854, and 727.

STITCHES

Lazy Daisy

Stem Stitch

INSTRUCTIONS

1. Transfer a weather design to each piece of white fabric and embroider.

2. Sew the aqua and white squares of fabric together end to end with ½-inch (1.3 cm) seams and press flat.

3. Pin the two strips of fabric together right sides facing and double-stitch along the edge ½ inch (1.3 cm) in. Start sewing along the top edge and leave a 2-inch (5.1 cm) space open at the end. Turn it right side out.

yellow orange
Stem Stitch

yellow
Stem Stitch

medium aqua
Stem Stitch

All-Weather Draft Dodger

INSTRUCTIONS CONTINUED

4. Fill the pillow with pellets. You can fill the bottom half with pellets and stuff the top half with fiberfill stuffing to give it a nice shape. Stitch the opening closed.

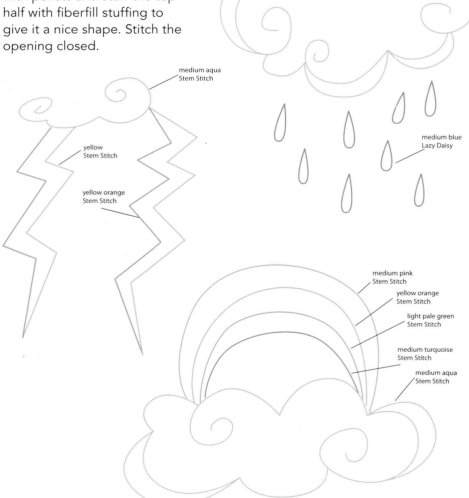

medium aqua
Stem Stitch

medium aqua
Stem Stitch

yellow
Stem Stitch

yellow orange
Stem Stitch

medium blue
Lazy Daisy

medium pink
Stem Stitch

yellow orange
Stem Stitch

light pale green
Stem Stitch

medium turquoise
Stem Stitch

medium aqua
Stem Stitch

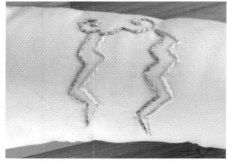

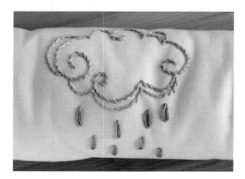

Happy Day Flag Banner

This fun, colorful flag banner is perfect for any celebration,
or just to brighten up a room.

Happy Day Flag Banner

WHAT YOU NEED

Templates (page 128)

½ yard (45.7 cm) each of pink, yellow, and orange fabric

Embroidery floss, 1 skein each of dark orange, medium orange, yellow, dark pink, and medium pink*

Orange ribbon, 2 pieces, each ¾ inch (1.9 cm) wide and 60 inches (152.4 cm) long

Motifs: 001, 004, 008, 016, 025, 115, 119, 121

The author used DMC embroidery floss colors 720, 721, 727, 760, and 761.

STITCHES

Back Stitch

Chain Stitch

French Knot

Lazy Daisy

Satin Stitch

Scallop Stitch

Split Stitch

INSTRUCTIONS

1. Transfer the templates to the fabric as shown, four pink, four orange, and three yellow.

2. Size the letter designs to 2½ inches (6.4 cm) tall and the crowns to 2 inches (5.1 cm) tall. Transfer the designs to the flag shapes and embroider.

3. Cut out each flag shape leaving ½ inch (1.3 cm) around the edges. Cut out a matching shape for the back of each flag. You can use the same fabric, or make a reversible banner by using different, patterned fabrics for the flag backs.

4. Pin the front and back of each flag together with right sides facing, and sew along the template lines, leaving the flag tops open. Trim the points as shown on page 25, turn each flag right side out, and press.

5. Stretch out the ribbons one on top of the other. Measuring in 12 inches (30.5 cm) from the end, start pinning the flags in order with the tops caught between the ribbons.

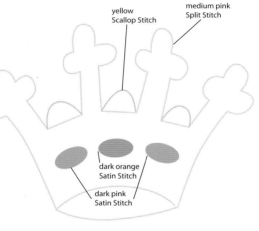

yellow
Scallop Stitch

medium pink
Split Stitch

dark orange
Satin Stitch

dark pink
Satin Stitch

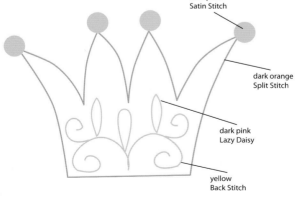

dark pink
Satin Stitch

dark orange
Split Stitch

dark pink
Lazy Daisy

yellow
Back Stitch

dark orange
Satin Stitch

light pink
French Knot

yellow
Split Stitch

dark pink
Split Stitch

6. Sew along the bottom edge and the top edge of the ribbons across all the flags. Tie up your banner and have a Happy Day!

dark orange
Chain Stitch

dark pink
Chain Stitch

yellow
Chain Stitch

medium orange
Chain Stitch

dark pink
Chain Stitch

dark orange
Chain Stitch

dark pink
Chain Stitch

yellow
Chain Stitch

Fabric Basket

This washable basket is the perfect size to hold little treasures. It hides a stiff, removable insert in the bottom, so when you're not using it, just untie the corners and store it away flat!

WHAT YOU NEED

Patterned yellow cotton fabric:
1 piece, 8¼ inches (21 cm)
square
2 pieces, each 11½ inches
(29.2 cm) square

Water-soluble fabric marker

Embroidery floss, 1 skein each
of dark coral, medium coral, and
light coral*

Peach satin ribbon, 8 pieces,
each 6 inches (15.2 cm) long

Heavy cardboard or hardboard,
7 ½ inches square (19 cm)

Motifs: 171 and 204

*The author used DMC embroidery
floss colors 351, 352, and 353.*

STITCHES

Chain Stitch

Running Stitch

Satin Stitch

Split Stitch

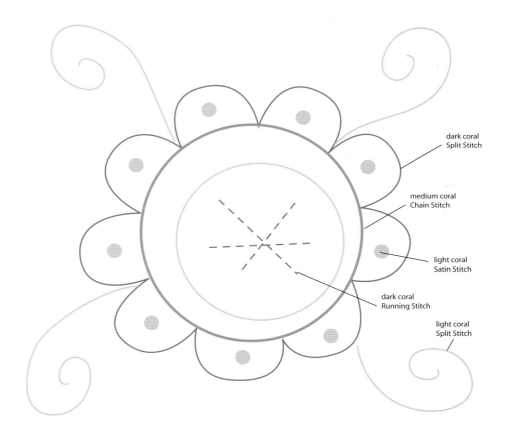

dark coral
Split Stitch

medium coral
Chain Stitch

light coral
Satin Stitch

dark coral
Running Stitch

light coral
Split Stitch

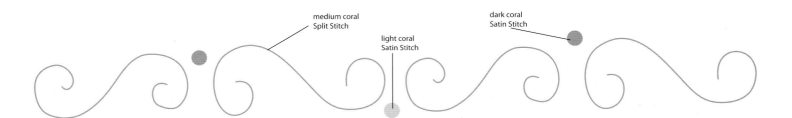

medium coral
Split Stitch

light coral
Satin Stitch

dark coral
Satin Stitch

Fabric Basket

INSTRUCTIONS

1. Mark an 8-inch (20.3 cm) square in the center of each large piece of fabric with a water-soluble fabric marker. Size the flower motif to 4 ¾ inches (12 cm) and transfer it to the center of one piece of fabric. Size the swirl border to 7 ½ inches (19 cm) and transfer one to each outside edge of the square on the second piece of fabric.

2. Embroider the designs using the Split Stitch for the outlines and the Satin Stitch for the dots.

3. Press ¼ inch (.6 cm) under on each edge of the small square of fabric. Hem one edge, and then center the square onto the larger fabric piece between the borders and sew the remaining three edges down. This will form a pocket that you will slide the cardboard insert into to keep the bottom stiff.

4. Place the two fabric pieces together with right sides facing. Make sure the two 8-inch (20.3 cm) squares you marked at the centers line up and pin them together. Now, measuring 1½ inches (3.8 cm) out from the 8-inch (20.3 cm) square, and mark an 11-inch (27.9 cm) square around the outside. Measure in 1½ inches (3.8 cm) from each corner in both directions and make a mark. You will sew a piece of the ribbon into the seam at each point (figure 1).

5. Sew the two pieces together on the 11-inch (27.9 cm) square line, leaving a 2-inch (5.1 cm) space open at the end to turn it.

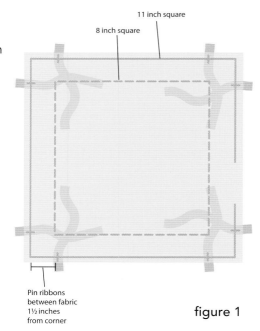

11 inch square

8 inch square

Pin ribbons between fabric 1½ inches from corner

figure 1

6. Turn the piece right side out and press the edges and corners flat. Now topstitch the 8-inch (20.3 cm) square around the center, and 1/8 inch (.3 cm) in around the outer edge (figure 2). Rinse out the basket to remove the fabric marker lines.

7. When the tray is dry, press it again, and insert the cardboard or hardboard in the back pocket. Now fold up the edges and tie each corner, forming a tray.

VARIATION

Use the cheerful sun motif on page 118 or one of the flower motifs on page 95-97.

Use the cheerful sun motif on page 118 or one of the flower motifs on page 95-97.

Tip

You can make these baskets in all different sizes. They are cheerful, colorful accessories for holding jewelry, office materials, or craft supplies.

Topstitch on these lines

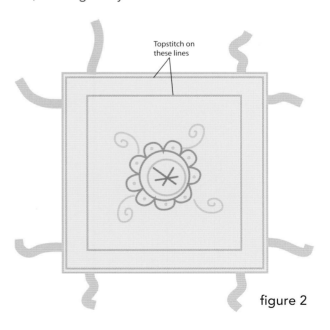

figure 2

Early Bird Lounge Pants

Whether you're an early bird or a night owl, you'll love these easy-to-make, cute and cozy flannel pants. Make them in any size using a pattern based on a pair of pants you already own.

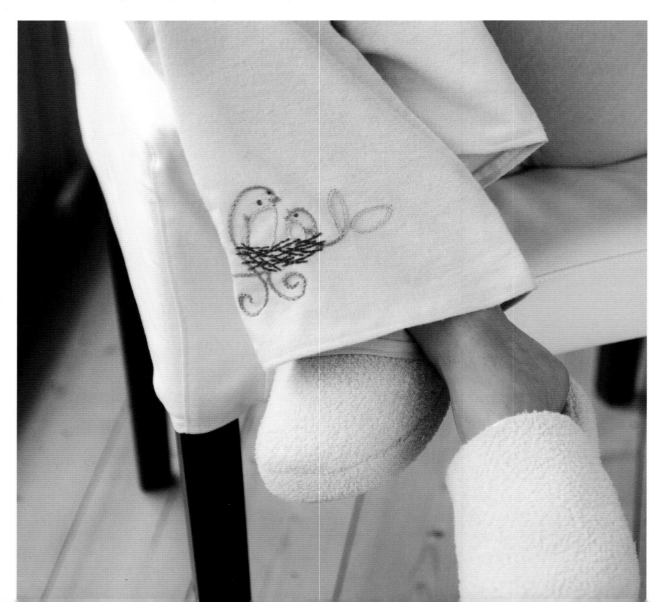

WHAT YOU NEED

Pair of lounge/pajama pants your size

2 yards (182.8 cm) of light blue flannel (1 yard [91.4 cm] may be enough for a child's pants)

1 package of ½-inch (1.3 cm) wide elastic

Large safety pin

Embroidery floss, 1 skein each of medium turquoise, light turquoise, pale green, dark brown, and medium brown*

Motif: 415

The author used DMC embroidery floss colors 597, 598, 3348, 433, and 435.

STITCHES

Back Stitch

Satin Stitch

Split Stitch

INSTRUCTIONS

1. You will be using your pair of pants to make a pattern. Fold your pants in half long ways, pulling the crotch out (figure 1). Fold the flannel so that it is large enough to cover the folded pants. Place the pants on the fold as shown and cut out 1 inch (2.5 cm) around the edge, leaving 2 inches (5.1 cm) extra at the top and bottom. Repeat for the other leg.

2. Fold each leg piece with right sides facing and sew the sides from ankle to crotch.

3. Turn one leg right side out and put it inside the other leg, lining up the seams. Pin the crotch sections together and sew from crotch to hip on both sides.

4. Pull the leg back out leaving the pants wrong side out. Now you will want to try on the pants and decide how much waist hem you want. Fold and pin down the waist at least 1 inch (2.5 cm) all the way around. I like the hem a bit higher in the back than the front. Sew the waist hem down ¾ inch (1.9 cm) from the fold, leaving a 2-inch (5.1 cm) opening at the end.

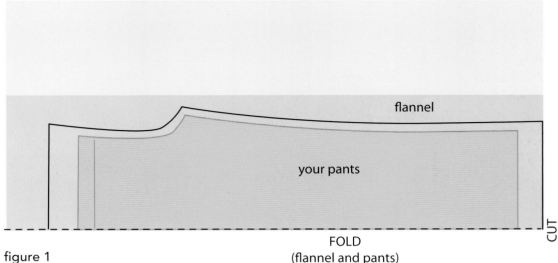

figure 1

flannel

your pants

CUT

FOLD
(flannel and pants)

Early Bird Lounge Pants

INSTRUCTIONS CONTINUED

5. Measure a piece of elastic long enough to fit around your waist, make a mark there, and then add 2 inches (5.1 cm). Attach a large safety pin to one end and thread it through the waistline.

6. Pull both ends out through the opening and sew them together on the line you marked. Cut off the excess and let the elastic go inside the waistline. Sew the opening closed.

7. Fold up each ankle cuff ½ inch (1.3 cm), then ½ inch (1.3 cm) again, then pin and sew the hems.

8. Turn the pants right side out, size the embroidery pattern to 6 x 3 inches (15.2 x 7.6 cm), and transfer it to one leg. Embroider the design.

VARIATION

The phases of the moon or star motifs (page 106) work well on this dreamy project.

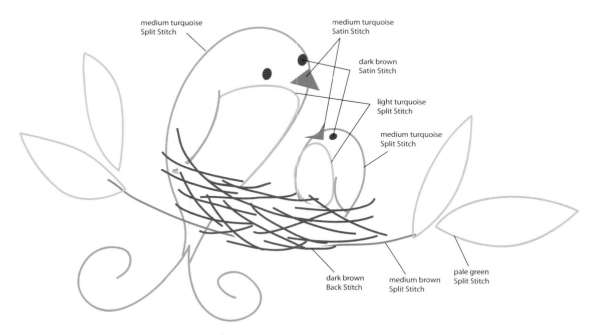

medium turquoise Split Stitch

medium turquoise Satin Stitch

dark brown Satin Stitch

light turquoise Split Stitch

medium turquoise Split Stitch

dark brown Back Stitch

medium brown Split Stitch

pale green Split Stitch

Satin Drawstring Gift Bags

These bags make luxurious wrapping for a special gift, and are an extra gift themselves.

Satin Drawstring Gift Bags

WHAT YOU NEED

Aqua satin fabric, 2 circles, each 8½ inches (21.6 cm)

Coral satin fabric, 2 circles, each 14 inches (35.6 cm)

Lavender satin fabric, 2 pieces, each 12 x 14 inches (30.5 x 35.6 cm)

Embroidery floss, 1 skein each of light pale green, medium coral, dark blue, medium blue, light blue, medium plum, and light plum*

Satin ribbon, ½ inch (1.3 cm) wide:
1 piece, 15 inches (38.1 cm) long
2 pieces, each 20 inches (50.8 cm) long

Large safety pin
Motifs: 114, 251, 308

The author used DMC embroidery floss colors 3348, 351, 340, 157, 3747, 3835, and 3836.

STITCHES

Back Stitch

Satin Stitch

Split Stitch

INSTRUCTIONS

1. Size the stars pattern to 1½ x 1½ inches (3.8 x 3.8 cm), the roses to 2½ x 3 inches (6.4 x 7.6 cm), and the grapes and wine pattern to 3 x 4 inches (7.6 x 10.2 cm), and transfer the designs to the fabric. For the small bag, position the design 2 inches (5.1 cm) from the edge. For the medium bag, position the design 3½ inches (8.9 cm) from the edge. For the wine bag, position the design 3 inches (7.6 cm) from the bottom, in the center. Embroider the designs according to the patterns.

2. For the circular bags, pin the two circles of fabric together with right sides facing. Starting right above the embroidered design, sew around the edge ½ inch (1.3 cm) in, leaving a 1-inch (2.5 cm) opening at the end. Turn it right side out and press the seams.

3. Now top-sew around the edge, ¾ inch (1.9 cm) in from the side.

4. Pin the safety pin to one end of the ribbon and thread it through the space around the edge of the circle. Pull both ends through the opening and tie them in a bow with your gift inside.

5. For the wine bag, fold each piece of fabric long ways with the right sides facing and sew ½ inch (1.3 cm) in along the long edge. Fold the tube so that the embroidery is in the front and the seam is along the back, and sew ½ inch (1.3 cm) in along the bottom. Pinch the corners flat and sew 1 inch (2.5 cm) in across each corner and trim off the extra point of fabric.

6. Turn the lining piece right side out and put it inside the outer piece (wrong side out), lining up the seams. Pin around the top edge. Starting directly above the embroidery, sew ½ inch (1.3 cm) in around the top edge, leaving a 1-inch (2.5 cm) opening at the end. Turn the entire bag right side out and push the lining down inside the outer bag.

7. Repeat steps 3 and 4.

VARIATION

Use motifs that suit your needs. For a baby shower, try any of the motifs on pages 79-80, or for a wedding favor, use mirror images of a bird motif from page 90.

medium coral
Back Stitch

light pale green
Back Stitch

medium blue
Satin Stitch

medium blue
Back Stitch

light blue
Back Stitch

medium plum
Split Stitch

light blue
Split Stitch

light pale green
Split Stitch

light plum
Back Stitch

Party Time Gift Tags

These fun tags will add a special handmade touch to any gift.

WHAT YOU NEED

Templates (page 125)

Heavy watercolor paper or cardstock, 2 x 3 inches (5.1 x 7.6 cm) for each tag

Craft knife

Hole punch

Embroidery floss, 1 skein each of light orange, medium pink, and light turquoise*

Satin ribbon, 6 inches (15.2 cm) for each tag

Motifs: 101, 104, 109

*The author used DMC embroidery floss colors 722, 761, and 598.

STITCHES

Back Stitch

French Knot

Lazy Daisy

Scallop Stitch

INSTRUCTIONS

1. Trace the tag templates onto the paper, then transfer the party motif to the paper using a light table or transfer paper.

2. Cut out the tag with a craft knife. You can use a hole punch to make the hole.

3. Split your strand of floss in half and use three of the six threads for this project. Start stitching the design just as you would on fabric. If you have trouble getting the needle to come up in the right place from the underside of the paper, try punching holes through from the top first.

4. Tie the ribbon through the hole and onto your package.

VARIATION

Use one of the fruits and veggies motifs on pages 101-103 to embellish a gifted potted plant, canned treat, or a packet of heirloom seeds.

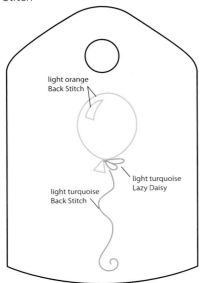

light orange
Back Stitch

light turquoise
Lazy Daisy

light turquoise
Back Stitch

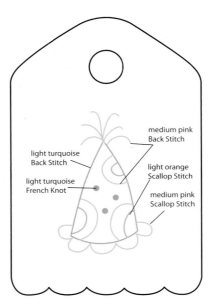

medium pink
Back Stitch

light turquoise
Back Stitch

light orange
Scallop Stitch

light turquoise
French Knot

medium pink
Scallop Stitch

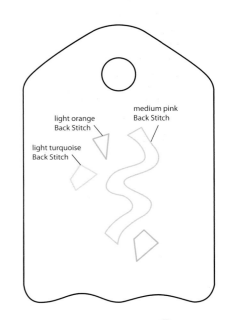

light orange
Back Stitch

medium pink
Back Stitch

light turquoise
Back Stitch

Snow Day Hat and Mittens

You'll be wishing for snow every day just so you can wear this cozy set.

WHAT YOU NEED

Tissue paper

Sticky back, tear-away fabric stabilizer

Knit hat and mittens

Embroidery floss, 1 skein of white*

Motifs: 401, 402, 403

The author used DMC embroidery floss in Blanc.

STITCHES

Back Stitch

French Knot

Satin Stitch

INSTRUCTIONS

1. Size the snowflake motifs to 1½ inches (3.8 cm) wide, trace them onto tissue paper, and cut them out.

2. Cut pieces of fabric stabilizer large enough to cover each design and apply them to the inside of the hat and each mitten.

3. Position the tissue paper patterns on the outside of each knit piece and pin them in place. You'll have the knit fabric sandwiched between a layer of tissue paper and stabilizer.

4. Begin embroidering the designs right through the layers of paper and fabric. On this project it's okay to not pull your stitches quite as tightly as you normally would, as you want to make sure the paper doesn't tear.

5. When you're finished embroidering, tear away the tissue paper and stabilizer. You can use a needle or some tweezers to carefully pull the paper out from under your stitches.

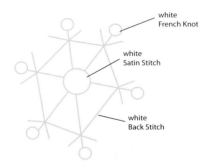

white French Knot

white Satin Stitch

white Back Stitch

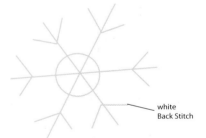

white Back Stitch

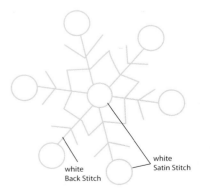

white Back Stitch

white Satin Stitch

Hoop-Framed Embroidery Art

Wooden embroidery hoops are perfect for framing your finished work. This pretty trio will add style to any room.

WHAT YOU NEED

Light tan cotton fabric

Lavender cotton fabric

Embroidery floss, 2 skeins each of dark plum, medium plum, light plum, 1 skein each of dark brown and medium brown*

1 6-inch (15.2 cm) wooden embroidery hoop

2 4-inch (10.2 cm) wooden embroidery hoops

Purple and brown satin ribbon, ⅜ to ⅝ inch (.95 to 1.6 cm) wide

White craft glue

Motifs: 163, 418, 419

*The author used DMC embroidery floss colors 3834, 3835, 3836, 433, and 435.

STITCHES

Frrench Knot

Satin Stitch

Split Stitch

Straight Stitch

INSTRUCTIONS

1. Measure and mark a 6-inch (15.2 cm) circle and two 4-inch (10.2 cm) circles on the fabric and cut them out, leaving at least 1 inch (2.5 cm) extra around the edge. Size the large henna design to 5 x 5 inches (12.7 x 12.7 cm) and the butterfly and moth designs to 3 inches (7.6 cm) wide.

medium plum
Split Stitch

light plum
Satin Stitch

light plum
SplitStitch

dark plum
SplitStitch

medium plum
Straight Stitch

dark plum
Split Stitch

Hoop-Framed Embroidery Art

INSTRUCTIONS CONTINUED

Transfer the embroidery designs to the fabric and stitch according to the pattern.

2. Stretch each piece tightly onto the wooden frames. Trim the edges of the fabric so there is about ½ inch (1.3 cm) left, and fold this over the back of the inner frame, gluing it down.

3. When the glue is dry, remove the outer frame of each hoop. Starting at the screw, angle the ribbon about 45° and wrap it around the frame tightly, gluing it down as you go.

4. Now replace the outer frames onto the inner hoops and embroidery, tighten the hoops, and hang your work up on the wall.

VARIATION

The sky is the limit here. Create your own wall art using any of the motifs in this book to suit almost every taste. Just size the designs to fit your available hoop frames.

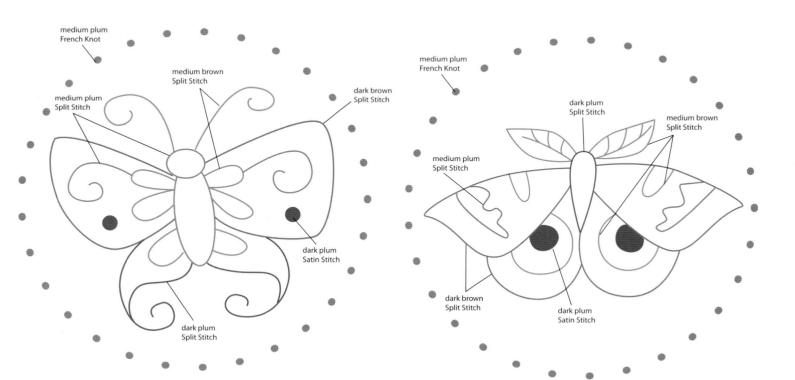

Sweet Shoppe Party Napkins and Rings

Colorful napkins add fun to any celebration, and napkins made from slap bracelets are just downright innovative. When you give them as party favors, you'll be the life of the party!

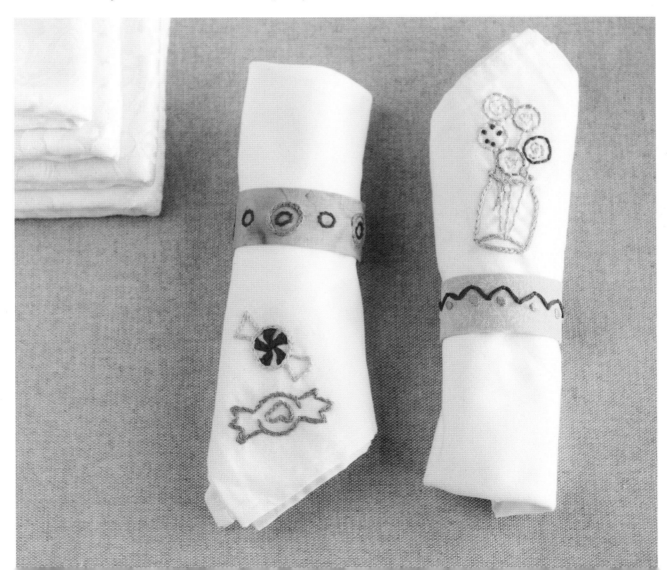

Sweet Shoppe Party Napkins and Rings

WHAT YOU NEED

White cotton or linen fabric, 1 piece for each napkin, 16 inches square (40.6 cm)

Pink or aqua fabric, 1 piece for each napkin ring, 9½ x 2¼ inches (24.1 x 5.7 cm)

Embroidery floss, 1 skein each of medium turquoise, light turquoise, light yellow brown, cherry red, dark pink, and medium pink*

Slap bracelet, 1 for each napkin ring, 9 x 1 (22.9 x 2.5 cm) inches

Motifs: 175, 176, 311, 320

The author used DMC embroidery floss colors 597, 598, 422, 304, 760, and 761.

STITCHES

Back Stitch

French Knot

Satin Stitch

Scallop Stitch

Split Stitch

INSTRUCTIONS

1. Press under the sides of each napkin ¼ inch (.6 cm), then ¼ inch (.6 cm) again to hide the raw edges, then sew.

2. Size the candy pattern to 2 x 2½ inches (5.1 x 6.4 cm), the lollipop jar pattern to 1½ x 3 inches (3.8 x 7.6 cm), and the border patterns to ½ inch (1.3 cm) wide. Transfer the candy designs to one corner of each napkin and the border designs to the center of each colored strip of fabric, and embroider them according to the pattern.

3. For each napkin ring, fold the colored fabric strip in half long ways with the right sides facing in. Sew ¼ inch (.6 cm) in around the edge, leaving one short side open.

4. Turn it right side out and press it flat with the embroidered design on top and the seam along the back.

5. If possible, remove any existing fabric and glue from the slap bracelet. Straighten it out and slide it inside the fabric casing you made. Tuck the open short side's ends in and hand-stitch it closed.

6. Wrap the bracelet/napkin rings around your folded napkins and set a festive party table!

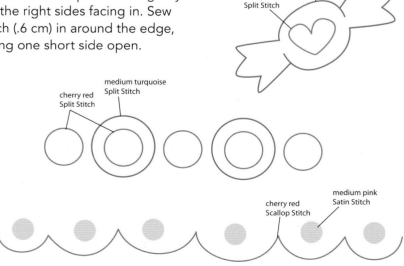

VARIATION

Hosting a sushi party? Use the cherry blossoms or ginko leaves on page 78. What about a festive celebration? Try the fireworks on page 87.

cherry red Split Stitch

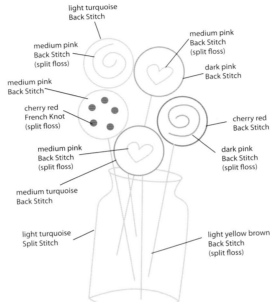

light turquoise Back Stitch

medium pink Back Stitch (split floss)

medium pink Back Stitch (split floss)

dark pink Back Stitch

medium pink Back Stitch

cherry red French Knot (split floss)

cherry red Back Stitch

medium pink Back Stitch (split floss)

dark pink Back Stitch (split floss)

medium turquoise Back Stitch

light turquoise Split Stitch

light yellow brown Back Stitch (split floss)

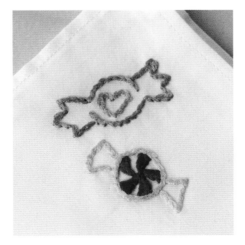

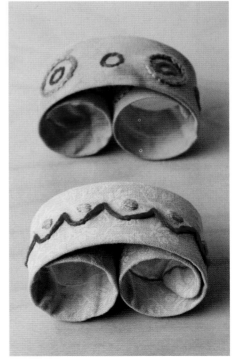

Sakura Parasol

Cherry blossoms are known as sakura in Japan, and they symbolize beauty and love. What a perfect embellishment for a pretty parasol!

WHAT YOU NEED

Silk or nylon parasol

Liquid or water-soluble fabric stabilizer

Embroidery floss, 1 skein each of dark pink, medium pink, and light brown*

Motif: 078

The author used DMC embroidery floss colors 760, 761, and 436.

STITCHES

Satin Stitch

Split Stitch

Straight Stitch

INSTRUCTIONS

1. Size the cherry blossom motif to 3¼ inches (8.3 cm) wide. You will need mirror images of this design.

2. Measure the area you will be embroidering and apply fabric stabilizer to the back of the fabric before you transfer the design, so your lines don't wash away in the process. If you're using liquid stabilizer, paint it on and let it dry. If you have a water-soluble paper stabilizer, wet the fabric and press pieces firmly onto the back. Let it dry completely.

3. Transfer the design to the fabric using a light box and pencil or transfer paper. Don't use the iron-on transfer method, and don't use a fabric marker—it will bleed and be difficult to see clearly. Transfer one design onto the fabric, and then transfer the flipped version so that the ends of the branches meet.

4. Split your floss in half and use three of the six threads for this design. When you're done stitching, rinse the fabric thoroughly with water to remove the stabilizer. Parasols make beautiful home or party decorations hung from the ceiling, or the perfect accessory for a beautiful bride or flower girl.

VARIATION

Stitch a raining cloud (page 117) on one side of the parasol and a sun or rainbow (pages 117-118) on the other.

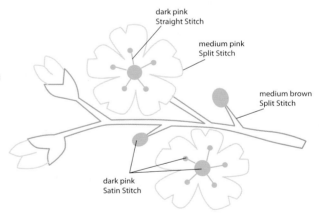

dark pink
Straight Stitch

medium pink
Split Stitch

medium brown
Split Stitch

dark pink
Satin Stitch

Double Reversible
Pop-Out Pillow

This uniquely designed pillow is not only different on either side, but it also has an insert that is reversible. Changing your décor is as easy as flipping either part around.

WHAT YOU NEED

Tissue paper

Aqua felt:
1 piece, 12 inches square
(30.5 cm)
1 circle, 8½ inches (21.6 cm)

Orange felt:
1 piece, 12 inches square
(30.5 cm)
1 circle, 8½ inches (21.6 cm)

Embroidery floss, 2 skeins each
of dark orange, light orange,
medium turquoise, and medium
aqua*

Polyester fiberfill stuffing

Motifs: 165, 169, 178, 184

*The author used DMC embroidery
floss colors 720, 722, 597, and 3811.*

STITCHES

Back Stitch

Lazy Daisy

Satin Stitch

Split Stitch

INSTRUCTIONS

1. Size the orange border design
to 4 inches (10.2 cm) wide, the blue
border design to 4½ inches (11.4
cm) wide, and each center design
to 5½ inches (14 cm) wide. Trace
them onto tissue paper, making four
copies of each border piece. Pin
the center designs securely to the
middle of each felt circle and the
border designs to the corners of the
felt squares, 1¼ inches (3.2 cm) from
the edge.

2. Embroider the designs and then
remove the tissue paper.

3. Measure a 5½-inch (14 cm) circle
in the center of each felt square and
cut it out. Pin the squares together
with right sides facing and sew ¼
inch (.6 cm) in around the edge,
leaving a 2-inch (5.1 cm) opening.
Turn it right side out and stitch the
opening closed.

Double Reversible Pop-Out Pillow

INSTRUCTIONS CONTINUED

4. Now sew the circle in the center by hand, stuffing the shape as you go.

5. Pin the two embroidered circles together with right sides facing and sew ½ inch (1.3 cm) in, leaving 2 inches (5.1 cm) open at the end to turn it right side out again. Stuff it firmly and sew up the opening.

6. The circle pillow insert will fit tightly inside the hole in the square pillow. You can turn it either way around and change it on a whim.

VARIATION

Create the perfect accent to a child's room with rocket ships (page 106) or whimsical circus designs (pages 85-87).

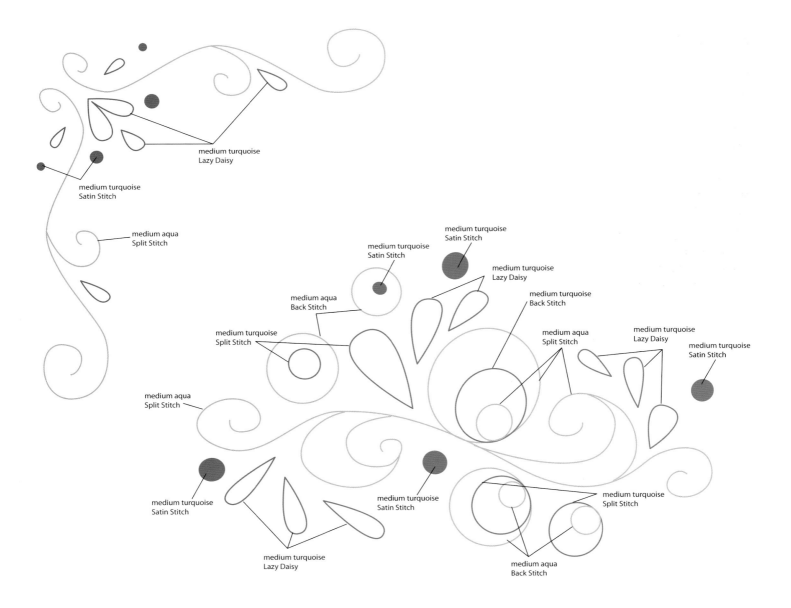

medium turquoise
Lazy Daisy

medium turquoise
Satin Stitch

medium aqua
Split Stitch

medium turquoise
Satin Stitch

medium turquoise
Satin Stitch

medium turquoise
Lazy Daisy

medium aqua
Back Stitch

medium turquoise
Back Stitch

medium turquoise
Split Stitch

medium aqua
Split Stitch

medium turquoise
Lazy Daisy

medium turquoise
Satin Stitch

medium aqua
Split Stitch

medium turquoise
Satin Stitch

medium turquoise
Split Stitch

medium turquoise
Satin Stitch

medium turquoise
Lazy Daisy

medium aqua
Back Stitch

Soft Sculpture Trio

These freestanding trees make a lovely arrangement for any shelf or mantle. No forest is complete without cute woodland animals, so stitch up a little detachable squirrel and bird to live there, too.

WHAT YOU NEED

Templates (pages 126-127)

Tissue paper

Aqua cotton fabric

Light green cotton fabric

Light yellow cotton fabric

Aqua felt

Light green felt

Moss green felt

Light yellow felt

Light brown felt

Embroidery floss, 1 skein each of medium turquoise, medium aqua, medium brown, dark brown, medium pale green, dark pale green, medium coral, light brown, and ecru*

Plastic beanbag pellets, dry rice, or beans

Polyester fiberfill stuffing

2 pin backs

Motifs: 340, 341, 357, 420, 428, 434

The author used DMC embroidery floss colors 597, 3811, 435, 433, 3347, 3346, 351, 437 and ecru.

STITCHES

Back Stitch

Chain Stitch

French Knot

Long and Short Stitch

Running Stitch

Satin Stitch

Split Stitch

Stem Stitch

Straight Stitch

INSTRUCTIONS

For the Trees:

1. Size the tree templates and embroidery designs as shown on pages 126-127, and cut out the pieces from the fabric and felt.

2. First stitch the large circular felt pieces in place on the green and aqua trees, then transfer the embroidery designs to each tree shape. Use the tissue paper method for the embroidery that goes over the felt parts.

3. Embroider the designs according to the pattern. Cut out the felt leaves and circles, and stitch them in place as shown.

4. For each tree, pin the front and back pieces together with right sides facing. Leave the bottom open, as well as a 2-inch (5.1 cm) opening on one side.

5. Pin a felt oval to the bottom of each tree and double-stitch it on. I find it easier to pin on the front half, sew it on, then pin and sew the back half. Now snip the seam edges and turn the tree right side out.

6. Fill the bottom 2 inches (5.1 cm) of the tree with beanbag pellets or dry rice or beans. Stuff the rest of the tree with fiberfill stuffing and stitch the opening closed.

Soft Sculpture Trio

INSTRUCTIONS CONTINUED

For the Animals:

1. Size the squirrel and bird motifs to 2½ inches (6.4 cm) wide and trace them onto tissue paper. Pin the paper to brown and aqua felt and embroider the designs.

2. Place another matching piece of felt behind each design and cut out each one leaving ¾ inch (1.9 cm) around the embroidery.

3. Hand-sew the two pieces of felt together with a bit of stuffing inside.

4. Stitch a pin back to the back of each one. Your bird and squirrel can hop from tree to tree.

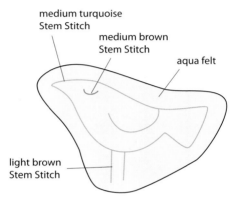

medium turquoise
Stem Stitch

medium brown
Stem Stitch

aqua felt

light brown
Stem Stitch

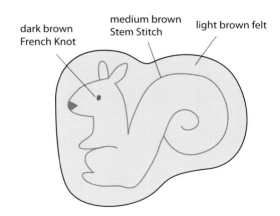

dark brown
French Knot

medium brown
Stem Stitch

light brown felt

Farmer's Market Tote Bag

Who needs paper or plastic when you have this fun, re-usable bag?
You'll be proud to tote this bag to the market.

Farmer's Market Tote Bag

WHAT YOU NEED

Canvas tote bag

Embroidery floss, 1 skein each of orange, dark orange, yellow, pink, red, light green, medium green, dark green, dark plum*

Motifs: 201, 203, 204, 205, 258, 268, 271, 275, 276, 277, 278, 279, 280, 283, 284, 285

The author used DMC embroidery floss colors 721, 722, 727, 761, 321, 907, 906, 905, and 3834.

STITCHES

French Knot

Lazy Daisy

Satin Stitch

Split Stitch

Straight Stitch

INSTRUCTIONS

1. Arrange vegetable and flower motifs in a square shape 7 inches (17.8 cm) wide.

2. Transfer the design to the fabric using any of the methods described on pages 12-13.

3. Hoop the fabric and embroider the design.

VARIATION

This project would be just as sweet using a grid of flower motifs on pages 95-97.

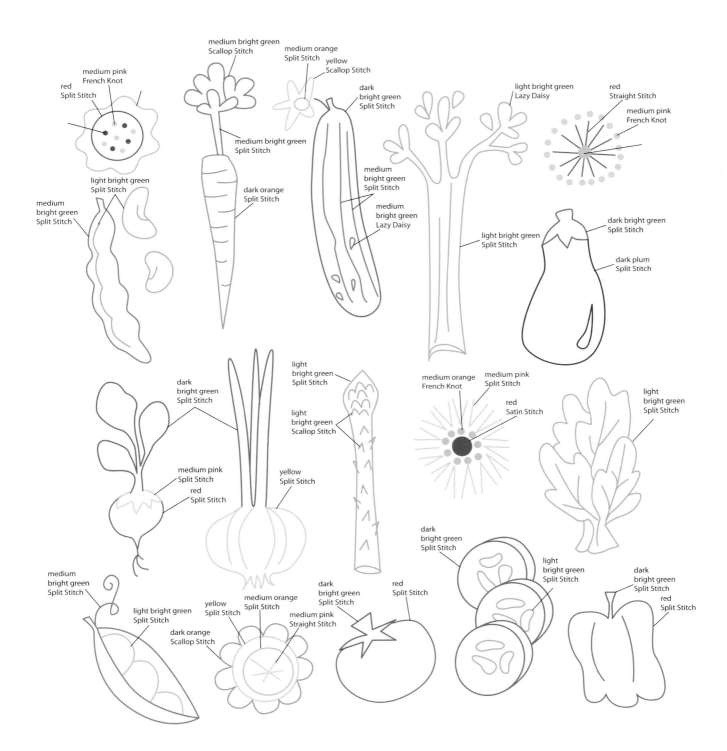

red
Split Stitch

medium pink
French Knot

medium bright green
Scallop Stitch

medium orange
Split Stitch

yellow
Scallop Stitch

dark
bright green
Split Stitch

light bright green
Lazy Daisy

red
Straight Stitch

medium pink
French Knot

medium
bright green
Split Stitch

light bright green
Split Stitch

medium bright green
Split Stitch

dark orange
Split Stitch

medium
bright green
Split Stitch

medium
bright green
Lazy Daisy

light bright green
Split Stitch

dark bright green
Split Stitch

dark plum
Split Stitch

dark
bright green
Split Stitch

light
bright green
Split Stitch

light
bright green
Scallop Stitch

medium orange
French Knot

medium pink
Split Stitch

red
Satin Stitch

light
bright green
Split Stitch

medium pink
Split Stitch

red
Split Stitch

yellow
Split Stitch

medium
bright green
Split Stitch

light bright green
Split Stitch

yellow
Split Stitch

medium orange
Split Stitch

dark
bright green
Split Stitch

red
Split Stitch

dark
bright green
Split Stitch

light
bright green
Split Stitch

dark
bright green
Split Stitch

red
Split Stitch

dark orange
Scallop Stitch

medium pink
Straight Stitch

A Walk in the Woods Wooden Charms

Embroider directly onto soft balsa wood to make these unique, versatile charms.

WHAT YOU NEED

Templates, page 125

½-inch (1.3 cm) thick balsa wood, at least 1½ inches (3.8 cm) wide, length based on the number of charms you plan to cut from it

Craft knife

Carbon paper

White craft glue

Cotton fabric

Embroidery floss, 1 skein each of medium turquoise, light turquoise, light pale green, medium pale green, and medium brown*

Pin backs

Ribbon, ½ inch (1.3 cm) wide and ⅛ inch (.3 cm) wide

Motifs: 224, 346, 417

*The author used DMC embroidery floss colors 597, 598, 3348, 3347, and 435.

STITCHES

Back Stitch

Blanket Stitch

French Knot

Lazy Daisy

Running Stitch

Satin Stitch

Star Stitch

Straight Stitch

Whip Stitch

INSTRUCTIONS

1. For each charm, trace the charm template onto wood and cut it out. Balsa wood is fairly easy to cut with a craft knife, but don't push too hard. Instead make several light cuts until you cut all the way through. To make a hole at the top of the charm for hanging, try using an awl or a seam ripper.

2. Now transfer the embroidery patterns to the charms using carbon paper. You may notice the lines starting to rub off as you begin to stitch; if this happens, trace over them with a pencil.

3. Spread a thin layer of white glue onto the back of the wood piece and glue it to the fabric. When it's dry, trim the extra fabric from around the edges. Small sewing scissors work best for this. The fabric will prevent the wood from cracking while you stitch.

A Walk in the Woods Wooden Charms

INSTRUCTIONS CONTINUED

4. Embroider the designs just as you would fabric, using three of the six threads. You will want to make holes from the front with your needle to be sure you're coming up at the right spot from the back. Hold the wood piece securely with two fingers on either side of the hole you're making as you stitch.

5. Glue your charms onto pin backs, or thread ribbon through the holes. You might find threading the ribbon through a large needle first will make this easier. To make the loop at the top of a charm, thread a ¾-inch (1.9 cm) length of the thinner ribbon through and glue both ends to the back. For the choker or bracelet, slide a piece of ½-inch (1.3 cm) ribbon through each slot from the back.

NOTE
Thin strips of balsa wood are available at many craft and hobby retailers.

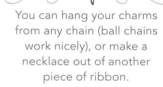

Tip

You can hang your charms from any chain (ball chains work nicely), or make a necklace out of another piece of ribbon.

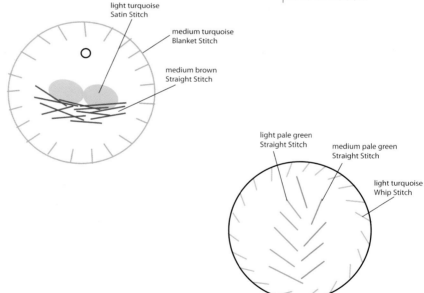

light turquoise
Satin Stitch

medium turquoise
Blanket Stitch

medium brown
Straight Stitch

light pale green
Straight Stitch

medium pale green
Straight Stitch

light turquoise
Whip Stitch

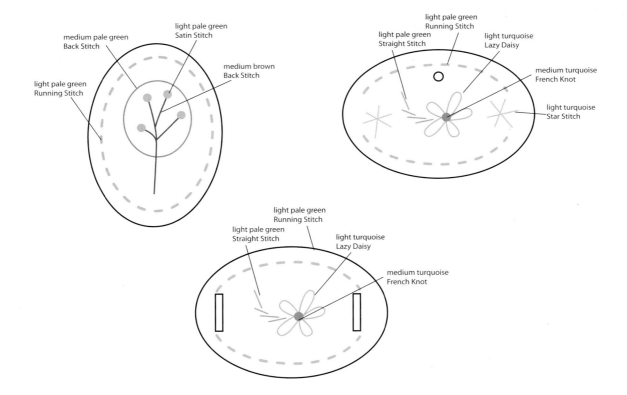

medium pale green
Back Stitch

light pale green
Satin Stitch

medium brown
Back Stitch

light pale green
Running Stitch

light pale green
Running Stitch

light pale green
Straight Stitch

light turquoise
Lazy Daisy

medium turquoise
French Knot

light turquoise
Star Stitch

light pale green
Running Stitch

light pale green
Straight Stitch

light turquoise
Lazy Daisy

medium turquoise
French Knot

Alphabet

Doodle

A 001 B 002 C 003 D 004 E 005 F 006

G 007 H 008 I 009 J 010 K 011 L 012

M 013 N 014 O 015 P 016 Q 017 R 018

S 019 T 020 U 021 V 022 W 023 X 024

Y 025 Z 026 a 027 b 028 c 029 d 030

e 031 f 032 g 033 h 034 i 035 j 036

k 037 l 038 m 039 n 040 o 041 p 042

q 043 r 044 s 045 t 046 u 047 v 048

w 049 x 050 y 051 z 052

Asian Chic

053

054

055

056

057

058

059

060

061

062

063

064

065

066

067

068

069

070

071

072

073

074

075

076

077

078

079

080

081

082

Baby

083

084

085

086

087

088

Baby

089

090

091

092

093

094

095

096

Celebrations

097

098

099

100

101

102

103

104

Celebrations

105

106

107

108

109

110

111

112

113

114

115

116

117

118

119

120

121

122

123

124

125

126

Celebrations

127

128

129

130

131

132

133

134

135

Circus

136

137

138

139

140

141

Circus

142

143

144

145

146

147

148

149

150

151

152

153

154

155

Embellishments

156

157

158

159

160

161

162

163

164

165

166

Embellishments

167

168

169

170

171

172

173

174

175

176

177

178

179

180

181

182

183

Embellishments

184

185

186

187

188

189

190

Farm Animals

191

192

193

194

195

Farm Animals

196

197

198

199

200

Flowers

201

202

203

204

205

206

207

208

209

210

Flowers

211

212

213

214

215

216

217

218

219

220

221

222

223

224

225

226

227

228

229

230

231

Food

232

233

234

235

236

237

238

239

240

241

242

243

244

245

246

247

248

Food

249

250

251

252

253

254

255

256

Fruits & Veggies

257

258

259

260

261

262

263

Fruits & Veggies

264

265

266

267

268

269

270

271

272

273

274

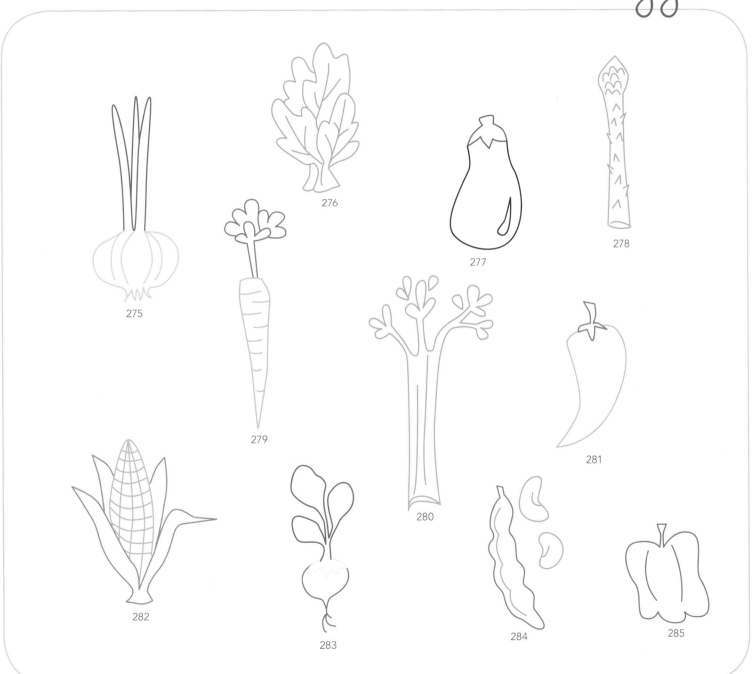

275

276

277

278

279

280

281

282

283

284

285

Garden Time

286

287

288

289

290

291

292

Space

293

294

295

296

297

298

299

Space

300

301

302

303

304

305

306

307

308

309

310

Sweet Shoppe

311

312

313

314

315

316

317

Sweet Shoppe

318

319

320

321

322

323

324

325

326

327

328

329

330

331

332

333

334

335

336

337

338

339

Trees & Leaves

340

341

342

343

344

345

346

347

Trees & Leaves

348

349

350

351

352

353

354

355

356

357

358

Under the Sea

359

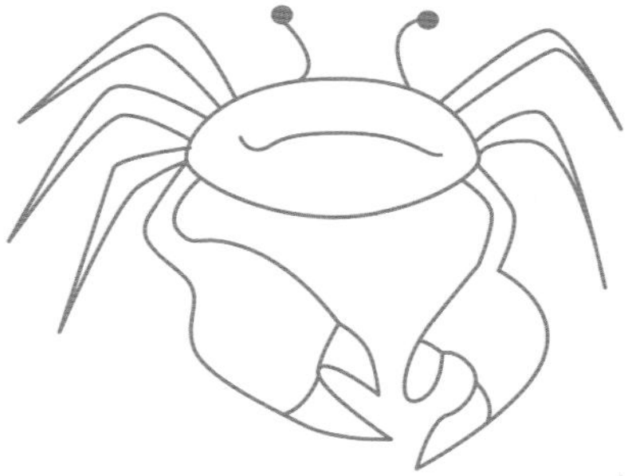

360

361

362

363

364

365

366

367

368

369

370

371

372

373

374

375

376

377

Under the Sea

378

379

380

381

382

383

384

385

386

387

388

389

Weather

390

391

392

393

394

395

Weather

396

401

397

398

399

400

402

403

404

405

406

Winged Wonders

407

408

409

410

411

412

413

414

Winged Wonders

415

416

417

419

418

420

421

422

Woodland Animals

423

424

425

426

427

428

429

430

431

Woodland Fairytale

432

433

434

435

436

437

438

439

440

441

442

443

Woodland Fairytale

444

445

446

447

448

449

450

Templates

Party Time Gift Tags
(page 48)

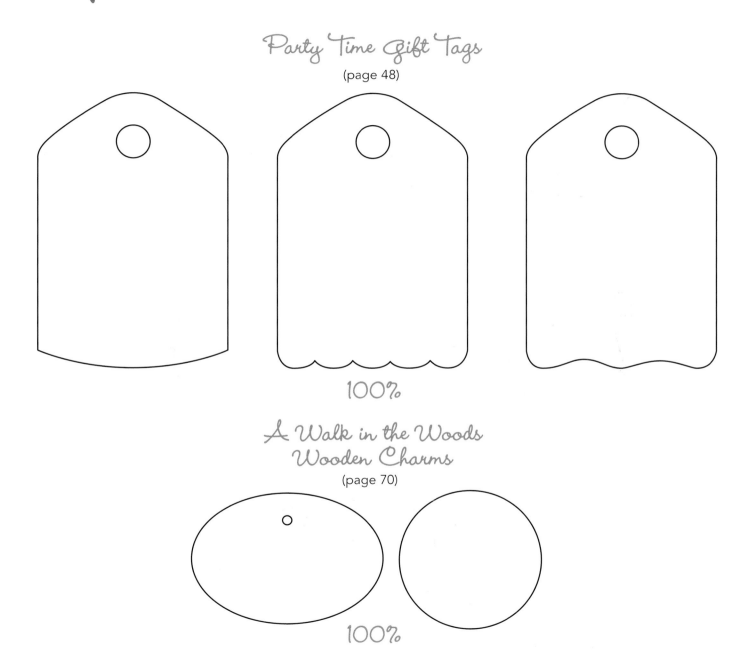

100%

A Walk in the Woods
Wooden Charms
(page 70)

100%

Soft Sculpture Trio
(page 64)

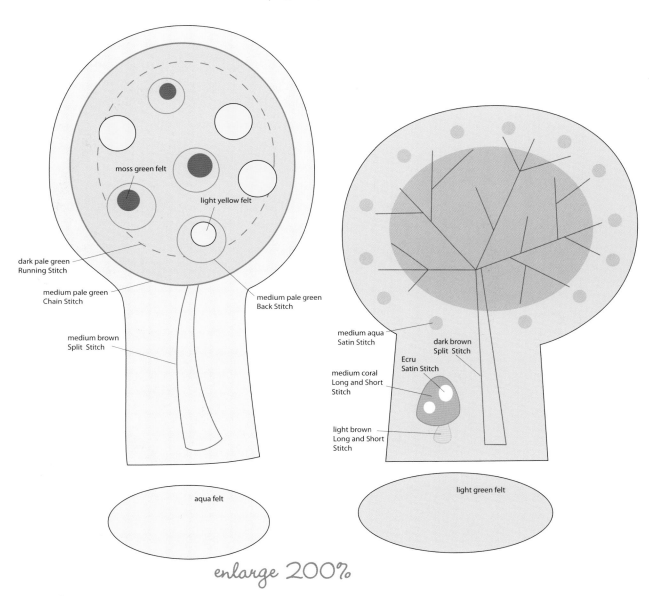

moss green felt

light yellow felt

dark pale green
Running Stitch

medium pale green
Chain Stitch

medium pale green
Back Stitch

medium brown
Split Stitch

medium aqua
Satin Stitch

dark brown
Split Stitch

Ecru
Satin Stitch

medium coral
Long and Short
Stitch

light brown
Long and Short
Stitch

aqua felt

light green felt

enlarge 200%

Soft Sculpture Trio

(page 64)

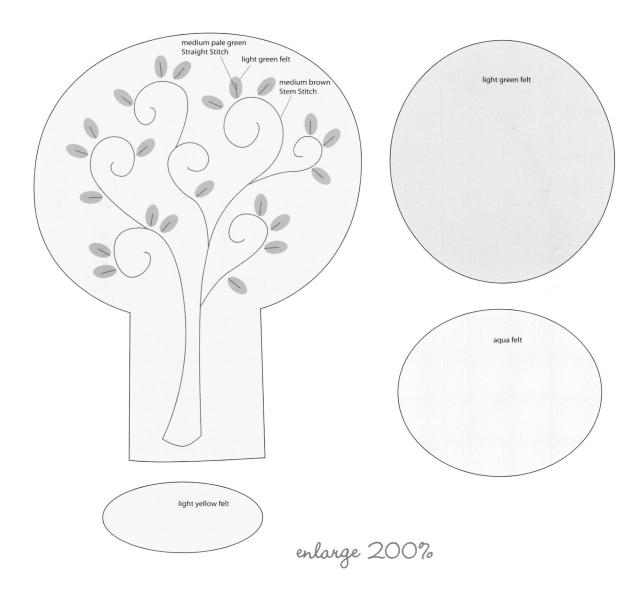

medium pale green
Straight Stitch

light green felt

medium brown
Stem Stitch

light green felt

aqua felt

light yellow felt

enlarge 200%

Happy Day Flag Banner

(page 35)

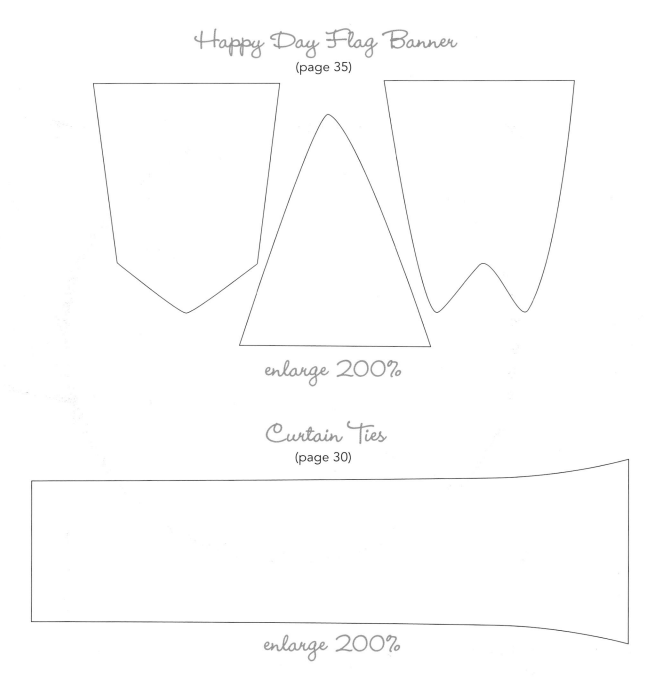

enlarge 200%

Curtain Ties

(page 30)

enlarge 200%

About the Author

Aimee Ray has been making things from paper, fabric, and clay for as long as she can remember. As a graphic designer in the greeting card and comic book industries, with several personal projects always in the works, she is almost never without something creative in hand, or in mind. Her diverse interests include digital painting and illustration, sewing, and embroidery. She is the author of the best-selling book *Doodle Stitching: Fresh & Fun Embroidery for Beginners* (Lark Books, 2007) and has contributed to many other Lark titles. You can see more of her work here: www.dreamfollow.com.

Acknowledgments

It's a lot of work to bring these ideas to life, and I am so grateful for the fun and challenging opportunity to create this book. Many thanks go to my husband, Josh, and my family, who always encourage me in everything I do. Thanks to my mom, grandma, and creative aunties who brought me up on a healthy diet of crafting.

I applaud my ace editorial team, Nicole and Beth, for helping direct the book with encouragement and experience. And I'm delighted with the art team of Kathy, Carol, Abby, and Dana, as well as photographer Lynne, for creating the perfect visual showcase for my work.

Thank you, Dana Dini, for knitting the perfect hat and mittens on page 50. The instructions for the pajama pants (page 42) were adapted from a tutorial on www.instructables.com.

I'm inspired every day by so many fellow designers. Here is a list of a few of my current favorites:

www.andreazuill.com

www.carolinehwangillustration.com

www.diemchau.com

www.jennyhart.net

www.lisasolomon.com

www.mimilove.net

Index

Find the stitch guide to this doodle stitch on
www.larkbooks.com/bonus